THE ANGLICAN ROSARY
ANGLICAN PRAYER BEADS
A FORM OF CONTEMPLATIVE PRAYER

Bibliografische Information der Deutschen Nationalbibliothek: Die Deutsche Nationalbibliothek verzeichnet diese Publikation in der DeutschenNationalbibliografie; detaillierte bibliografische Daten sind im Internet über http//dnb.dnb.de abrufbar.

Bibliographic information published by the Deutsche Nationalbibliothek The Deutsche Nationalbibliothek lists this publication in the Deutsche Nationalbibliografie; detailed bibliographic data are available on the Internet at http://dnb.dnb.de.

Informazione bibliografica della Deutsche Nationalbibliothek La Deutsche Nationalbibliothek registra questa pubblicazione nella Deutsche Nationalbibliografie; dettagliati dati bibliografici sono disponibili in internet in http://dnb.dnb.de.

Imprimatur:
Mons. Dr. F. Haas
Anglican (Extra) Province of Christ the Saviour &
Anglican Catholic Diocese of Christ the Redeemer

Publishing house: St. Alcuin of York Anglican Publishers http://apubli.org
Printing and production: BoD - Books on Demand, Norderstedt/Germany
ISBN: 978-3-945233-08-5 (Hardcover)
Printed in Germany

CONTENT

INTRODUCTION

The use of the rosary or prayer beads helps to bring us into contemplative of meditative prayer – really thinking about and being mindful of praying, of being in the presence of God – by use of mind, body, and spirit. The touching of the fingers on each successive bead is an aid in keeping our mind from wandering, and the rhythm of the prayers leads us more readily into stillness.

Symbolism of the Beads

The configuration of the Anglican Prayer Beads relate contemplative prayer using the Rosary to many levels of traditional Christian symbolism. Contemplative prayer is enriched by these symbols whose purpose is always to focus and concentrate attention, allowing the one who prays to move more swiftly into the Presence of God.

The prayer beads are made up of twenty-eight beads divided into four groups of seven called weeks. In the Judeo-Christian tradition the number seven represents spiritual perfection and completion. Between each week is a single bead, called a cruciform bead as the four beads form a cross. The invitatory bead between the cross and the wheel of beads brings the total to thirty-three, the number of years in Jesus' earthly life.

Praying with the beads

To begin, hold the Cross and say the prayer you have assigned to it, then move to the Invitatory Bead. Then enter the circle of the prayer with the first Cruciform Bead, moving to the right, go through the first set of seven beads to the next Cruciform bead, continuing around the circle, saying the prayers for each bead.

It is suggested that you pray around the circle of the beads three times (which signifies the Trinity) in an unhurried pace, allowing the repetition to become a sort of lullaby of love and praise that enables your mind to rest and your heart to become quiet and still.

Praying through the beads three times and adding the crucifix at the beginning or the end, brings the total to one hundred, which is the total of the Orthodox Rosary. A period of silence should follow the prayer, for a time of reflection and listening. Listening is an important part of all prayer.

Begin praying the Anglican Prayer Beads by selecting the prayers you wish to use for the cross and each bead. Practice them until it is clear which prayer goes with which bead, and as far as possible commit the prayers to memory.

Find a quiet spot and allow your body and mind to become restful and still. After a time of silence, begin praying the prayer beads at an unhurried, intentional pace. Complete the circle of the beads three times.

When you have completed the round of the prayer beads, you should end with a period of silence. This silence allows you to center your being in an extended period of silence. It also invites reflection and listening after you have invoked the Name and Presence of God.

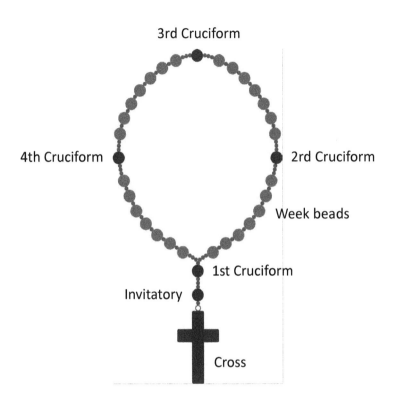

3rd Cruciform

4th Cruciform

2rd Cruciform

Week beads

1st Cruciform

Invitatory

Cross

Prayer of Intercession

Cross

Our Father, who art in heaven, hallowed be thy name;
thy kingdom come; thy will be done; on earth as it is in heaven.
Give us this day our daily bread. And forgive us our trespasses,
as we forgive those who trespass against us.
And lead us not into temptation; but deliver us from evil.
For thine is the kingdom, and the power and the glory,
for ever and ever. Amen.

Invitatory

Glory be to the Father, and to the Son, and to the Holy Spirit;
As it was in the beginning, is now, and ever shall be,
world without end. Amen.

Cruciform

Let your way be known upon earth, *
your saving health among all nations.
Let not the needy, O Lord, be forgotten, *
nor the hope of the poor be taken away.

Versicles, Daily Office

Weeks

So bless our loved ones, our enemies, and ourselves
that our need may be met, our suffering eased,
and our heart made whole in the perfect love
of your Son Jesus Christ. Amen.

Prayer for Confidence in God

Cross
Our Father, who art in heaven, hallowed be thy name;
thy kingdom come; thy will be done; on earth as it is in heaven.
Give us this day our daily bread. And forgive us our trespasses,
as we forgive those who trespass against us.
And lead us not into temptation; but deliver us from evil.
For thine is the kingdom, and the power and the glory,
for ever and ever. Amen.

Invitatory
Glory be to the Father, and to the Son, and to the Holy Spirit;
As it was in the beginning, is now, and ever shall be,
world without end. Amen.

Cruciform
This is another day, O Lord. I know not what it will bring forth,
but make me ready, Lord, for whatever it may be.
If I am to stand up, help me to stand bravely. If I am to sit still,
help me to sit quietly. If I am to lie low, help me to do it pa-
tiently. And if I am to do nothing, let me do it gallantly.
Make these words more than words, and give me the Spirit of
Jesus. Amen.

Weeks
Why are you so full of heaviness, O my soul? *
and why are you so disquieted within me?
Put your trust in God, for I will yet give thanks to him, *

who is the help of my countenance, and my God.
Psalm 42:14-15

MORNING PRAYER (FORM 1)

Cross
Let the words of my mouth and the meditation of my heart
be acceptable in your sight, O Lord, my strength and my
redeemer.
Psalm 19:14

Invitatory
Lord, open my lips,
and my mouth shall proclaim your praise.

Cruciform
Come let us sing to the Lord; *
let us shout for joy to the Rock of our salvation.
Let us come before his presence with thanksgiving *
and raise a loud shout to him with psalms.
Come, let us bow down, and bend the knee, *
and kneel before the Lord our Maker.
For he is our God,
and we are the people of his pasture and the sheep of his hand.*
Oh, that today you would hearken to his voice! *Psalm 97:1-2,6-7*
or the entirety of the Venite (see Book of Common Prayer p. 82), or the following
Glorify the Lord, all you works of the Lord, *
praise him and highly exalt him for ever.

In the firmament of his power, glorify the Lord, *
praise him and highly exalt him for ever.
Song of the Three Young Men

Weeks

Bless the Lord, O my soul, *
and all that is within me, bless his holy Name.
Psalm 103:1

Dismissary

The hour is coming, and now is, when the true worshipers
will worship the Father in spirit and truth,
for such the Father seeks to worship him.
John 4:23

Cross

Our Father, who art in heaven, hallowed be thy name;
thy kingdom come; thy will be done; on earth as it is in heaven.
Give us this day our daily bread. And forgive us our trespasses,
as we forgive those who trespass against us.
And lead us not into temptation; but deliver us from evil.
For thine is the kingdom, and the power and the glory,
for ever and ever. Amen.

Morning Prayer (Form 2)

Cross
Thus says the high and lofty One who inhabits eternity, whose name is Holy, „I dwell in the high and holy place and also with the one who has a contrite and humble spirit, to revive the spirit of the humble and to revive the heart of the contrite." *Isaiah 57:15*

Invitatory
Lord, open my lips,
and my mouth shall proclaim your praise.

Cruciform
Let the words of my mouth and the meditation of my heart be acceptable in your sight, *
O Lord, my strength and my redeemer. *Psalm 19:14*
or the following (omit "Alleluia" during Lent)
(Alleluia.) Christ our Passover has been sacrificed for us; *
therefore let us keep the feast,
not with the old leaven, the leaven of malice and evil, *
but with the unleavened bread of sincerity and truth. (Alleluia.)
1 Corinthians 5:7-8

Weeks
Early in the morning, Lord, you hear my voice; *
early in the morning I make my appeal
and watch for you. *Psalm 5:3*
or the following

Blessed be the Lord day by day, *
the God of our salvation, who bears our burdens.
Psalm 68:19

Dismissary

Send out your light and your truth, that they may lead me,
and bring me to your holy hill and to your dwelling.
Psalm 43:3

Cross

Our Father, who art in heaven, hallowed be thy name;
thy kingdom come; thy will be done; on earth as it is in heaven.
Give us this day our daily bread. And forgive us our trespasses,
as we forgive those who trespass against us.
And lead us not into temptation; but deliver us from evil.
For thine is the kingdom, and the power and the glory,
for ever and ever. Amen.

MORNING PRAYER (FORM 3 - PROTECTION)

Cross

The first word I say in the morning, when I arise:
May Christ's cross be my armor about me.

Invitatory

Lord, open my lips,
and my mouth shall proclaim your praise.

Cruciform

Help me, I beseech you,
since I am as if in peril on the great sea,
so that this year's plague does not drag me off,
nor the world's vanity…
O God, defend me everywhere
with your impregnable power and protection.
Deliver all my mortal limbs,
guarding each with your protective shield.

From The Breastplate of Laidcenn (a.d.661)

Weeks

I shall put on the Lord's protection today.
I shall arm myself splendidly;
He who created me shall give me strength.

or the following

Help me, Unity in Trinity.
Trinity in Unity, take pity.

From The Breastplate of Laidcenn (d.661)

Dismissary

God the Sender, send us. God the Sent, come with us.
God the Strengthener of those who go, empower us, that we may go with you and find those who will call you Father, Son, and Holy Spirit. Amen.

Cross

Our Father, who art in heaven, hallowed be thy name;
thy kingdom come; thy will be done; on earth as it is in heaven.

Give us this day our daily bread. And forgive us our trespasses,
as we forgive those who trespass against us.
And lead us not into temptation; but deliver us from evil.
For thine is the kingdom, and the power and the glory,
for ever and ever. Amen.

MORNING PRAYER (FORM 4 - PRAISE)

Cross
O Lord, grant me the skill to sing your praise,
for the bustle of this world is perilous.

Invitatory
Lord, open my lips,
and my mouth shall proclaim your praise.

Cruciform
Almighty Creator, it is you who made the land and the sea…
The world cannot comprehend in song bright and melodious,
even though all the grass and trees should sing
all your wonders, O true Lord!
The Father created the world by a miracle;
It is difficult to express its measure.
Clear and High and in perfect assembly,
let us praise above the nine orders of angels
the sublime and blessed Trinity.

Early Welsh Prayer

Weeks

Let us adore the Lord, maker of marvelous works;
Bright heaven with its angels,
and on earth the white-waved sea.

Old Irish, 9th century

or the following

Glory and honor and goodwill,
praise and sublime song of minstrels,
overflowing love from every heart
to the King of heaven and earth.

Irish, ninth century

Dismissary

Creator of the universe, watch over us and keep us in the
light of your presence. May our praise continually blend with
that of all creation, until we come together to the eternal joys
which you promise in love, through Jesus Christ our Lord.

Cross

Our Father, who art in heaven, hallowed be thy name;
thy kingdom come; thy will be done; on earth as it is in heaven.
Give us this day our daily bread. And forgive us our trespasses,
as we forgive those who trespass against us.
And lead us not into temptation; but deliver us from evil.
For thine is the kingdom, and the power and the glory,
for ever and ever. Amen.

Prayer at Noonday (Form 1)

Cross
If anyone is in Christ s/he is a new creation; the old has passed away, behold the new has come. All this is from God, who through Christ reconciled us to himself and gave us the ministry of reconciliation. *2 Corinthians 5:17-18*

Invitatory
Glory to the Father, and to the Son, and to the Holy Spirit;
As it was in the beginning, is now, and ever shall be,
world without end. Amen.

Cruciform
I lift up my eyes to the hills; *
from where is my help to come?
My help comes from the LORD, *
the maker of heaven and earth.
Psalm 121:1-2

or the following

From the rising of the sun to its setting my Name shall be great among the nations, and in every place incense shall be offered to my Name, and a pure offering; for my Name shall be great among the nations, says the Lord of Hosts.
Malachi 1:11

Weeks
Your word is a lantern to my feet *
and a light upon my path.

I am sworn and I am determined *
to keep your righteous judgments.

Psalm 119:105-106

Dismissary

Glory be to the Father, and to the Son, and to the Holy Spirit;
As it was in the beginning, is now, and ever shall be,
world without end. Amen.

Cross

Our Father, who art in heaven, hallowed be thy name;
thy kingdom come; thy will be done; on earth as it is in heaven.
Give us this day our daily bread. And forgive us our trespasses,
as we forgive those who trespass against us.
And lead us not into temptation; but deliver us from evil.
For thine is the kingdom, and the power and the glory,
for ever and ever. Amen.

PRAYER AT NOONDAY (FORM 2 - GUIDANCE)

Cross

Grant me, O Lord, the lamp of love which never grows dim,
that it may shine in me and warm my heart, and give light to
others through my love for them, and by its brightness we
may have a vision of the Holy City where the true and inex-
tinguishable light shines, Jesus Christ our Lord. Amen.

Columbanus, d. 615

Invitatory

Glory be to the Father, and to the Son, and to the Holy Spirit;
As it was in the beginning, is now, and ever shall be,
world without end. Amen.

Cruciform

Lord, be a bright flame before me, be a guiding star above me,
be a smooth path below me, be a kindly shepherd behind me,
today and for evermore. Amen.

Columba, d. 597.

Weeks

O Lord, work good in us, and provide us
with what you know we need. Amen.

Latin, attributed to Columbanus

or the following

Give us memory, give us love,
give us chastity, give us faith,
give us all things you know
belong to the profit of our soul. Amen.

Latin, attributed to Columbanus

Dismissary

O Lord God, sow understanding and good works in our
mouth and heart; so that in act and in truth we may serve
only you and know how to fulfill the commandments of
Christ and to seek yourself. Amen.

Latin, attributed to Columbanus

Cross
Our Father, who art in heaven, hallowed be thy name;
thy kingdom come; thy will be done; on earth as it is in heaven.
Give us this day our daily bread. And forgive us our trespasses,
as we forgive those who trespass against us.
And lead us not into temptation; but deliver us from evil.
For thine is the kingdom, and the power and the glory,
for ever and ever. Amen.

EVENING PRAYER (FORM 1)

Cross
Yours is the day, O God, yours also the night;
you established the moon and the sun.
You fixed all the boundaries of the earth;
you made both summer and winter.
Psalm 74:15,16

Invitatory
O God, make speed to save us;
O Lord, make haste to help us.

Cruciform
O gracious light,
pure brightness of the everliving Father in heaven,
O Jesus Christ, holy and blessed!
Now as we come to the setting of the sun,
and our eyes behold the vesper light,

we sing your praises, O God: Father, Son, and Holy Spirit.
You are worthy at all times to be praised by happy voices,
O Son of God, O Giver of life,
and to be glorified through all the worlds.

Phos Hilaron

or the entirety of the Phos Hilaron (see BCP p.118), or the following

Glorify the Lord, you angels and all powers of the Lord, *
O heavens and all waters above the heavens.
Sun and moon and stars of the sky, glorify the Lord, *
praise him and highly exalt him for ever.

Song of the Three Young Men, 37-41

Weeks

Let my prayer be set forth in your sight as incense, *
the lifting up of my hands as the evening sacrifice.

Psalm 141:2

Dismissary

I will bless the Lord who gives me counsel;
my heart teaches me, night after night.
I have set the Lord always before me;
because he is at my right hand, I shall not fall.

Psalm 16:7,8

Cross

Our Father, who art in heaven, hallowed be thy name;
thy kingdom come; thy will be done; on earth as it is in heaven.
Give us this day our daily bread. And forgive us our trespasses,
as we forgive those who trespass against us.

And lead us not into temptation; but deliver us from evil.
For thine is the kingdom, and the power and the glory,
for ever and ever. Amen.

EVENING PRAYER (FORM 2)

Cross
Seek him who made the Pleiades and Orion, and turns deep
darkness into the morning, and darkens the day into night;
who calls for the waters of the sea and pours them out upon
the surface of the earth: The Lord is his name.

Amos 5:8

Invitatory
O God, make speed to save us;
O Lord, make haste to help us.

Cruciform
Holy God,
Holy and Mighty,
Holy Immortal One,
Have mercy upon us.

Trisagion

or the following

O God, you will keep in perfect peace those whose minds are
fixed on you; for in returning and rest we shall be saved;
in quietness and trust shall be our strength.

Isaiah 26:3; 30:15

Weeks

Lord, you are in the midst of us and we are called by your
name: Do not forsake us, O Lord our God. Amen.

Jeremiah 14:9,22

or the following

Guide us waking, O Lord, and guard us sleeping;
That awake we may watch with Christ, and asleep we may
rest in peace. Amen.

Dismissary

If I say, „Surely the darkness will cover me, and the light
around me turn to night," darkness is not dark to you,
O Lord; the night is as bright as the day;
darkness and light to you are both alike.

Psalm 139:10, 11

Cross

Our Father, who art in heaven, hallowed be thy name;
thy kingdom come; thy will be done; on earth as it is in heaven.
Give us this day our daily bread. And forgive us our trespasses,
as we forgive those who trespass against us.
And lead us not into temptation; but deliver us from evil.
For thine is the kingdom, and the power and the glory,
for ever and ever. Amen.

Evening Prayer (Form 3)

Cross
O God make speed to save us.
O Lord make haste to help us.

Invitatory
As our evening prayer rises before you, O God,
so may your mercy come down upon us to cleanse our hearts
and set us free to sing your praise, now and forever. Amen.

Cruciforms
Let my prayer rise before you as incense,
the lifting up of my hands as the evening sacrifice.

Weeks
Lord have mercy,
Christ have mercy,
Lord have mercy.

Invitatory
The Grace of our Lord Jesus Christ, and the love of God,
and the fellowship of the Holy Spirit be with us all evermore.
Amen.

Cross
Let us bless the Lord, thanks be to God.

EVENING PRAYER (FORM 4)

Cross
Glory be to the Father, and to the Son, and to the Holy Spirit;
As it was in the beginning, is now, and ever shall be,
world without end. Amen.

Invitatory
Open my lips, O Lord,
and my mouth shall proclaim Your praise.

Cruciforms
Guide us waking, O Lord,
and guard us sleeping;
that awake we may watch with Christ,
and asleep we may rest in peace.

Weeks
Jesus, lamb of God, have mercy on us.
Jesus, bearer of our sins, have mercy on us.
Jesus, redeemer of the world, give us your peace

EVENING PRAYER (FORM 5)

Cross
Yours is the day, O God, yours also the night;
you established the moon and the sun.
You fixed all the boundaries of the earth;

you made both summer and winter.

Psalm 74:15,16

Invitatory

O God, make speed to save us;
O Lord, make haste to help us. Amen.

Cruciform

May your holy angels, O Christ, son of the living God,
tend our sleep, our rest, our bright bed.
Let them reveal true visions to us in our sleep,
O High Prince of the universe, O great and mysterious King.
May no demons, no evil, no injury or terrifying dreams
disturb our rest, our prompt and swift repose.
May our waking, our work, and our living be holy;
our sleep, our rest, without hindrance or harm.

(attributed to Patrick; Irish, 9th century or earlier)

Weeks

Glorify the Lord, you angels and all powers of the Lord, *
O heavens and all waters above the heavens.
Sun and moon and stars of the sky, glorify the Lord, *
praise him and highly exalt him for ever.

Song of the Three Young Men, 37-41

or the following

Creator of the universe, watch over us and keep us
in the light of your presence.

Dismissary

You are my strength, Lord, I will love you.
Under the shadow of your wings protect me.

From The Prayers of Moucan, Welsh, 8th century

Cross

Our Father, who art in heaven, hallowed be thy name;
thy kingdom come; thy will be done; on earth as it is in heaven.
Give us this day our daily bread. And forgive us our trespasses,
as we forgive those who trespass against us.
And lead us not into temptation; but deliver us from evil.
For thine is the kingdom, and the power and the glory,
for ever and ever. Amen.

COMPLINE (NIGHT PRAYER FORM 1)

Cross

Be sober, be watchful. Your adversary the devil prowls around
like a roaring lion, seeking someone to devour.
Resist him, firm in your faith.

1 Peter 5:8-9a

Invitatory

My help is in the Name of the Lord;
the maker of heaven and earth. Amen.

Cruciform

Lord, you now have set your servant free *

to go in peace as you have promised;
For these eyes of mine have seen the Savior, *
whom you have prepared for all the world to see:
A Light to enlighten the nations, *
and the glory of your people Israel.

Luke 2:29-32

or the following

O God, you will keep in perfect peace those whose minds are
fixed on you; for in returning and rest we shall be saved;
in quietness and trust shall be our strength.

Isaiah 26:3; 30:15

Weeks

Be our light in the darkness, O Lord, and in your great mercy
defend us from all perils and dangers of this night;
for the love of your only Son, our Savior Jesus Christ. Amen.

or the following

Guide us waking, O Lord, and guard us sleeping;
that awake we may watch with Christ, and asleep we may rest
in peace. Amen.

Dismissary

Come to me, all who labor and are heavy-laden, and I will
give you rest. Take my yoke upon you, and learn from me;
for I am gentle and lowly in heart, and you will find rest for
your souls. For my yoke is easy, and my burden is light.

Matthew 11:28-30

Cross

Our Father, who art in heaven, hallowed be thy name;
thy kingdom come; thy will be done; on earth as it is in heaven.
Give us this day our daily bread. And forgive us our trespasses,
as we forgive those who trespass against us.
And lead us not into temptation; but deliver us from evil.
For thine is the kingdom, and the power and the glory,
for ever and ever. Amen.

COMPLINE (NIGHT PRAYER FORM 2)

Cross

May your holy angels, O Christ, son of the living God,
tend our sleep, our rest, our bright bed.

Attributed to Patrick; Irish, 9th century or earlier

Invitatory

My help is in the Name of the Lord;
the maker of heaven and earth. Amen.

Cruciform

Be the peace of the Spirit mine this night,
be the peace of the Son mine this night,
be the peace of the Father mine this night,
the peace of all peace be mine this night,
each morning and evening of my life. Amen.

From Carmina Gadelica, trans. Alexander Carmichael

Weeks

May our waking, our work, and our living be holy;
our sleep, our rest, without hindrance or harm.

Attributed to Patrick; Irish, 9th century or earlier

Dismissary

O God, you will keep in perfect peace those whose minds are
fixed on you; for in returning and rest we shall be saved;
in quietness and trust shall be our strength.

Isaiah 26:3, 30:15

Cross

Our Father, who art in heaven, hallowed be thy name;
thy kingdom come; thy will be done; on earth as it is in heaven.
Give us this day our daily bread. And forgive us our trespasses,
as we forgive those who trespass against us.
And lead us not into temptation; but deliver us from evil.
For thine is the kingdom, and the power and the glory,
for ever and ever. Amen.

SEASONAL (HOLY WEEK)

Cross

All we like sheep have gone astray; we have turned every one
to his own way; and the Lord has laid on him the iniquity
of us all. *Isaiah 53:6*

Invitatory

Glory to the Father, and to the Son, and to the Holy Spirit;
As it was in the beginning, is now, and ever shall be,
world without end. Amen.

Cruciform

Save me, O God, *
for the waters have risen up to my neck.
I am sinking in deep mire, *
and there is no firm ground for my feet.
I have grown weary with my crying;
my throat is inflamed; *
my eyes have failed from looking for God.

Psalm 69: 1-2,4

or the following

 I gave my back to those who struck me,
and my cheeks to those who pulled out the beard; *
I did not hide my face from insult and spitting.
The Lord God helps me; *
therefore I have not been disgraced;
Therefore I have set my face like flint, *
and I know that I shall not be put to shame.

Isaiah 50:6-7

Weeks

Be not far away, O Lord; *
you are my strength; hasten to help me.

Psalm 22:18

Dismissary

Is it nothing to you, all you who pass by? Look and see
if there is any sorrow like my sorrow which was brought
upon me, whom the Lord has afflicted.

Lamentations 1:12

Cross

Our Father, who art in heaven, hallowed be thy name;
thy kingdom come; thy will be done; on earth as it is in heaven.
Give us this day our daily bread. And forgive us our trespasses,
as we forgive those who trespass against us.
And lead us not into temptation; but deliver us from evil.
For thine is the kingdom, and the power and the glory,
for ever and ever. Amen.

Seasonal (Lent)

Cross

I will arise and go to my father, and I will say to him,
„Father, I have sinned against heaven and before you;
I am no longer worthy to be called your child."

Luke 15:18-19

Invitatory

Glory be to the Father, and to the Son, and to the Holy Spirit;
As it was in the beginning, is now, and ever shall be,
world without end. Amen.

Cruciform

Now, O Lord, I bend the knee of my heart, *
and make my appeal, sure of your gracious goodness.
I have sinned, O Lord, I have sinned, *
and I know my wickedness only too well.
Therefore I make this prayer to you: *
Forgive me, Lord, forgive me.

Prayer of Manasseh 11-13

or the entire Prayer of Manasseh (BCP p. 90), or the following

Open my lips, O Lord, *
and my mouth shall proclaim your praise.
Had you desired it, I would have offered sacrifice, *
but you take no delight in burnt-offerings.
The sacrifice of God is a troubled spirit; *
a broken and contrite heart,
O God, you will not despise.

Psalm 150: 16-18

Weeks

Create in me a clean heart, O God, *
and renew a right spirit within me.

Psalm 50: 11

Dismissary

Rend your hearts and not your garments. Return to the Lord
your God, for he is gracious and merciful, slow to anger and
abounding in steadfast love, and repents of evil.

Joel 2:13

Cross

Our Father, who art in heaven, hallowed be thy name;
thy kingdom come; thy will be done; on earth as it is in heaven.
Give us this day our daily bread. And forgive us our trespasses,
as we forgive those who trespass against us.
And lead us not into temptation; but deliver us from evil.
For thine is the kingdom, and the power and the glory,
for ever and ever. Amen.

Seasonal (Advent)

Cross

In the wilderness prepare the way of the Lord, make straight
in the desert a highway for our God.

Isaiah 40:3

Invitatory

Glory be to the Father, and to the Son, and to the Holy Spirit;
As it was in the beginning, is now, and ever shall be,
world without end. Amen.

Cruciform

When the Lord restored the fortunes of Zion, *
then were we like those who dream.
Then was our mouth filled with laughter, *
and our tongue with shouts of joy.
Then they said among the nations, *
"The Lord has done great things for them."

The Lord has done great things for us,
and we are glad indeed.

Psalm 126:1-4

or the following

My soul proclaims the greatness of the Lord,
my spirit rejoices in God my Savior; *
for he has looked with favor on his lowly servant.
From this day all generations will call me blessed: *
the Almighty has done great things for me,
and holy is his Name.

Luke 1:46-49

Or the entirety of Psalm 126, or the Magnificat (see BCP p. 119)

Weeks

Show us your mercy, O Lord, *
and grant us your salvation.

Psalm 85:7

Dismissary

The glory of the Lord shall be revealed,
and all flesh shall see it together.

Isaiah 40:5

Cross

Our Father, who art in heaven, hallowed be thy name;
thy kingdom come; thy will be done; on earth as it is in heaven.
Give us this day our daily bread. And forgive us our trespasses,
as we forgive those who trespass against us.
And lead us not into temptation; but deliver us from evil.

For thine is the kingdom, and the power and the glory,
for ever and ever. Amen.

SEASONAL (CHRISTMAS)

Cross
Behold, the dwelling of God is with mankind. He will dwell
with them, and they shall be his people, and God himself
will be with them, and be their God.
Revelation 21:3

Invitatory
Glory be to the Father, and to the Son, and to the Holy Spirit;
As it was in the beginning, is now, and ever shall be,
world without end. Amen.

Cruciform
Behold, I bring you good news of a great joy which will
come to all the people; for to you is born this day in the city
of David, a Savior, who is Christ the Lord.
Luke 2:10, 11

or the following

The Word became flesh and dwelt among us, *
and we have seen his glory:
The glory as of a father's only son, *
full of grace and truth.
No one has ever seen God;
it is God the only Son *

who is near to the Father's heart,
who has made him known.

John 1:14,18

Weeks

Glory to God in the highest, *
and peace to his people on earth! Amen.

Luke 2:14

Dismissary

Light has sprung up for the righteous, *
and joyful gladness for those who are truehearted.
O give thanks unto the Lord, and call upon his Name; *
tell the people what he has done.

Psalm 97:11, 105:1

Cross

Our Father, who art in heaven, hallowed be thy name;
thy kingdom come; thy will be done; on earth as it is in heaven.
Give us this day our daily bread. And forgive us our trespasses,
as we forgive those who trespass against us.
And lead us not into temptation; but deliver us from evil.
For thine is the kingdom, and the power and the glory,
for ever and ever. Amen.

Seasonal (Epiphany)

Cross
Nations shall come to your light,
and kings to the brightness of your rising.
Isaiah 60:3

Invitatory
Glory be to the Father, and to the Son, and to the Holy Spirit;
As it was in the beginning, is now, and ever shall be,
world without end. Amen.

Cruciform
Lord, you now have set your servant free *
to go in peace as you have promised;
For these eyes of mine have seen the Savior, *
whom you have prepared for all the world to see:
A Light to enlighten the nations, *
and the glory of your people Israel.
Luke 2:29-32

or the following
Who can fail to do you homage, Lord,
and sing the praises of your Name? *
for you only are the Holy One.
All nations will draw near and fall down before you, *
because your just and holy works have been revealed.
Revelation 15:4

Or the entirety of The Song of the Redeemed (BCP)

Weeks

Blessed be the Lord God, the God of Israel, *
who alone does wondrous deeds!
And blessed be his glorious Name for ever! *
and may all the earth be filled with his glory.

Psalm 72:18-19

Dismissary

I will give you as a light to the nations,
that my salvation may reach to the end of the earth.

Isaiah 49:6b

Cross

Our Father, who art in heaven, hallowed be thy name;
thy kingdom come; thy will be done; on earth as it is in heaven.
Give us this day our daily bread. And forgive us our trespasses,
as we forgive those who trespass against us.
And lead us not into temptation; but deliver us from evil.
For thine is the kingdom, and the power and the glory,
for ever and ever. Amen.

PRAYERS OF PRAISE

Cross

Our Father, who art in heaven, hallowed be thy name;
thy kingdom come; thy will be done; on earth as it is in heaven.
Give us this day our daily bread. And forgive us our trespasses,
as we forgive those who trespass against us.
And lead us not into temptation; but deliver us from evil.
For thine is the kingdom, and the power and the glory,
for ever and ever. Amen.

Invitatory

Glory be to the Father, and to the Son, and to the Holy Spirit;
As it was in the beginning, is now, and ever shall be,
world without end. Amen.

Cruciform

Give praise, you servants of the LORD; *
praise the Name of the LORD.
Let the Name of the LORD be blessed, *
from this time forth for evermore.

Psalm 113:1-2

Weeks

Glory to you, Lord God of our fathers; *
you are worthy of praise; glory to you.
Glory to you for the radiance of your holy Name; *
we will praise you and highly exalt you for ever.

Song of the Three Young Men, 29-30

Prayers for Succor

Cross
Our Father, who art in heaven, hallowed be thy name;
thy kingdom come; thy will be done; on earth as it is in heaven.
Give us this day our daily bread. And forgive us our trespasses,
as we forgive those who trespass against us.
And lead us not into temptation; but deliver us from evil.
For thine is the kingdom, and the power and the glory,
for ever and ever. Amen.

Invitatory
Glory be to the Father, and to the Son, and to the Holy Spirit;
As it was in the beginning, is now, and ever shall be,
world without end. Amen.

Cruciform
Why are you so full of heaviness, O my soul? *
and why are you so disquieted within me?
Put your trust in God, for I will yet give thanks to him, *
who is the help of my countenance, and my God.

Psalm 42:14-15

Weeks
Have mercy on me, O Lord, for I am in trouble; *
my eye is consumed with sorrow,
and also my throat and my belly.

Psalm 31:9

PRAYER OF SELF-DEDICATION

Cross
Our Father, who art in heaven, hallowed be thy name;
thy kingdom come; thy will be done; on earth as it is in heaven.
Give us this day our daily bread. And forgive us our trespasses,
as we forgive those who trespass against us.
And lead us not into temptation; but deliver us from evil.
For thine is the kingdom, and the power and the glory,
for ever and ever. Amen.

Invitatory
Glory be to the Father, and to the Son, and to the Holy Spirit;
As it was in the beginning, is now, and ever shall be,
world without end. Amen.

Cruciform
Lord, make us instruments of your peace. *
Where there is hatred, let us sow love;
where there is injury, pardon; *
where there is discord, union;
where there is doubt, faith; *
where there is despair, hope;
where there is darkness, light; *
where there is sadness, joy.
attributed to St. Francis
or the following
Grant that we may not so much seek to be consoled as to
console;

to be understood as to understand;
to be loved as to love.
For it is in giving that we receive;
it is in pardoning that we are pardoned;
and it is in dying that we are born to eternal life.

Attr. to St. Francis

Weeks

O God, be all my love, all my hope, all my striving;
Let my thoughts and words flow from you,
my daily life be in you,
and every breath I take be for you. Amen.

John Cassian

PRAYERS FOR MERCY

Cross

Our Father, who art in heaven, hallowed be thy name;
thy kingdom come; thy will be done; on earth as it is in heaven.
Give us this day our daily bread. And forgive us our trespasses,
as we forgive those who trespass against us.
And lead us not into temptation; but deliver us from evil.
For thine is the kingdom, and the power and the glory,
for ever and ever. Amen.

Invitatory

Glory be to the Father, and to the Son, and to the Holy Spirit;
As it was in the beginning, is now, and ever shall be,

world without end. Amen.

Cruciform
Holy God,
Holy and Mighty,
Holy Immortal One,
Have mercy upon us.

Trisagion

Weeks
Jesus Christ, son of the Living God;
Have mercy upon me, a sinner. Amen.

Prayers for Godliness

Cross
Our Father, who art in heaven, hallowed be thy name;
thy kingdom come; thy will be done; on earth as it is in heaven.
Give us this day our daily bread. And forgive us our trespasses,
as we forgive those who trespass against us.
And lead us not into temptation; but deliver us from evil.
For thine is the kingdom, and the power and the glory,
for ever and ever. Amen.

Invitatory
Glory be to the Father, and to the Son, and to the Holy Spirit;
As it was in the beginning, is now, and ever shall be,
world without end. Amen.

Cruciform

Grant to us your servants that we may have,
to our God, a heart of flame;
To our neighbors, a heart of love; *
And to ourselves, a heart of steel.

St. Augustine of Hippo

Weeks

Let the words of my mouth and the meditation of my heart
be acceptable in your sight, O Lord, my strength and my
redeemer. *Psalm 19:14*

SEASONAL (EASTER SEASON)

Cross

If then you have been raised with Christ, seek the things that
are above, where Christ is, seated at the right hand of God.
Col. 3:1

Invitatory

Glory be to the Father, and to the Son, and to the Holy Spirit;
As it was in the beginning, is now, and ever shall be,
world without end. Amen.

Cruciform

Your right hand, O Lord, is glorious in might; *
your right hand, O Lord, has overthrown the enemy.
Who can be compared with you, O Lord, among the gods? *

who is like you, glorious in holiness,
awesome in renown, and worker of wonders?
You stretched forth your right hand; *
the earth swallowed them up.
With your constant love you led the people you redeemed; *
with your might you brought them in safety
to your holy dwelling.

Exodus 15:6,11-13

or the following

There is a sound of exultation and victory *
in the tents of the righteous:
„The right hand of the Lord has triumphed! *
the right hand of the Lord is exalted!
the right hand of the Lord has triumphed!"

Psalm 118:16

Weeks

Thanks be to God, who gives us the victory
through our Lord Jesus Christ. Amen.

1 Corinthians 15:57

Dismissary

Christ has entered, not into a sanctuary made with hands,
a copy of the true one, but into heaven itself, now to appear
in the presence of God on our behalf.

Hebrews 9:24

Cross

Our Father, who art in heaven, hallowed be thy name;
thy kingdom come; thy will be done; on earth as it is in heaven.
Give us this day our daily bread. And forgive us our trespasses,
as we forgive those who trespass against us.
And lead us not into temptation; but deliver us from evil.
For thine is the kingdom, and the power and the glory,
for ever and ever. Amen.

THE ANGELUS

Cross

Glory be to the Father, and to the Son, and to the Holy Spirit;
As it was in the beginning, is now, and ever shall be,
world without end. Amen.

Invitatory

We beseech you O Lord to pour your grace into our hearts,
that as we have known the incarnation of your Son Jesus
Christ by the message of an angel, so by His cross and
passion we may be brought to the glory of His resurrection.
Through Jesus Christ our Lord. Amen.

Cruciforms

The angel of the Lord brought tidings to Mary;
and she conceived by the Holy Spirit.
Behold the handmaid of the Lord;
let it be to me according to your word.

The word was made flesh and dwelt among us.
Pray for us O Holy mother of God that we may be made worthy of the promises of Christ.

Weeks
Hail Mary, full of grace, the Lord is with thee,
blessed art thou among women, and blessed is the fruit of thy womb, Jesus. Holy Mary, mother of God, pray for us sinners now and at the hour of our death.

COME LORD JESUS PRAYER

Cross
Blessing and glory and wisdom and thanksgiving and honor and power and might be to our God forever and ever! Amen.

Revelation 7:12

Invitatory
God is our refuge and strength,
a very present help in time of trouble.

Psalm 46:1

Cruciforms
Bless the Lord, O my soul, and all that is within me, bless God's Holy Name.

Psalm 103:1

Weeks
Come Lord Jesus, draw us to yourself. *John 12:32*

Franciscan Prayer

Cross
In the name of the creator, redeemer and sanctifier of life.
Amen.

Invitatory
We adore you most holy Lord Jesus Christ,
here and in all your Churches throughout the whole world,
and we bless you because by your holy cross
you have redeemed the world.

Cruciforms
Most high and glorious God, enlighten the darkness of our
hearts and give us true faith, a certain hope and a prefect love.
Give us a sense of the Divine and a knowledge of yourself,
so that we may do everything in fulfillment of your holy will.

Weeks
My God, my all.

Invitatory
May our blessed Lady pray for us.
May St Francis, St Clare and St Elizabeth pray for us.
May all the saints of God pray for us.

May the angels of God befriend us and watch around us to protect us. May the Lord Jesus give us his blessing of peace. Amen.

Cross
In the name of the creator, redeemer and sanctifier of life. Amen

TRISAGION AND JESUS PRAYER
Trisagion means „thrice Holy"

Cross
In the Name of God, Father, Son, and Holy Spirit. Amen.

Invitatory
O God make speed to save me (us),
O Lord make haste to help me (us),
glory to the Father, and to the Son, and to the Holy Spirit;
as it was in the beginning, is now, and ever shall be,
world without end. Amen.

Cruciforms
Holy God,
Holy and Mighty,
Holy Immortal One,
Have mercy upon me (us).

Weeks

Lord Jesus Christ, Son of God,

Have mercy on me, a sinner.

Or, in a group setting:

Lord Jesus Christ, Son of God, Have mercy upon us.

AGNUS DEI PRAYER

Agnus Dei means „Lamb of God"

Cross

Our Father, who art in heaven, hallowed be thy name;

thy kingdom come; thy will be done; on earth as it is in heaven.

Give us this day our daily bread. And forgive us our trespasses,

as we forgive those who trespass against us.

And lead us not into temptation; but deliver us from evil.

For thine is the kingdom, and the power and the glory,

for ever and ever. Amen.

Invitatory

Let the words of my mouth and the meditation of my heart

be acceptable in your sight, O Lord, my strength and my

redeemer. *Psalm 19:14*

Cruciforms

Oh, Lamb of God that taketh away the sins of the world

have mercy upon us,

Oh, Lamb of God that taketh away the sins of the world

have mercy upon us,

Oh, Lamb of God that taketh away the sins of the world
give us Thy Peace.

Weeks
Almighty and merciful Lord,
Father, Son, and Holy Spirit,
bless us and keep us. Amen.

JULIAN OF NORWICH PRAYER

Cross
In the Name of God, Father, Son, and Holy Spirit. Amen.

Invitatory
O God make speed to save me (us),
O Lord make haste to help me (us),
glory to the Father, and to the Son, and to the Holy Spirit;
as it was in the beginning, is now, and ever shall be,
world without end. Amen.

Cruciforms
God of your goodness, give me yourself,
for you are enough to me.
And I can ask for nothing less that is to your glory.
And if I ask for anything less, I shall still be in want,
for only in you have I all.

Weeks

All shall be well, and all shall be well,
and all manner of things shall be well.

or the following

In His love He has done His works,
and in His love He has made all things beneficial to us.

by Sister Brigit-Carol, S.D.

CELTIC PRAYER

Cross

In the Name of God, Father, Son, and Holy Spirit. Amen.

Invitatory

O God make speed to save me (us),
O Lord make haste to help me (us),
glory to the Father, and to the Son, and to the Holy Spirit;
As it was in the beginning, is now, and ever shall be,
world without end. Amen.

Cruciforms

Be the eye of God dwelling with me,
the foot of Christ in guidance with me,
the shower of the Spirit pouring on me,
richly and generously.

Weeks
Pray each phrase on a separate bead.
I bow before the Father who made me,
I bow before the Son who saved me,
I bow before the Spirit who guides me,
in love and adoration.
I praise the Name of the one on high.
I bow before thee Sacred Three,
the ever One, the Trinity.

by Sister Brigit-Carol, S.D

SAINT PATRICK'S BREASTPLATE

Cross
I bind unto myself today the strong Name of the Trinity,
by invocation of the same, the Three in One, and One in
Three.
Of whom all nature hath creation, eternal Father, Spirit, Word:
praise to the Lord of my salvation, salvation is of Christ the
Lord.

Invitatory
Christ be with me, Christ within me, Christ behind me,
Christ before me,
Christ beside me, Christ to win me, Christ to comfort and
restore me.
Christ beneath me, Christ above me, Christ in quiet, Christ
in danger,

Christ in hearts of all that love me, Christ in mouth of friend and stranger.

Cruciforms
I bind unto myself today
the strong Name of the Trinity,
by invocation of the same,
the Three in One, and One in Three.

Weeks
1. I bind this day to me for ever, by power of faith,
   Christ's incarnation;
2. his baptism in Jordan river;
3. his death on cross for my salvation;
4. his bursting from the spicèd tomb;
5. his riding up the heavenly way;
6. his coming at the day of doom:
7. I bind unto myself today

1. I bind unto myself the power of the great love of cherubim;
2. the sweet „Well done" in judgment hour;
3. the service of the seraphim;
4. confessors' faith, apostles' word,
5. the patriarchs' prayers, the prophets' scrolls;
6. all good deeds done unto the Lord,
7. and purity of virgin souls.

1. I bind unto myself today the virtues of the starlit heaven,
2. the glorious sun's life-giving ray,

3. the whiteness of the moon at even,
4. the flashing of the lightning free,
5. the whirling of the wind's tempestuous shocks,
6. the stable earth, the deep salt sea,
7. around the old eternal rocks.

1. I bind unto myself today the power of God
   to hold and lead,
2. his eye to watch, his might to stay,
3. his ear to hearken, to my need;
4. the wisdom of my God to teach,
5. his hand to guide, his shield to ward;
6. the word of God to give me speech,
7. his heavenly host to be my guard.

Words: attributed to St. Patrick (372-466) translated by Cecil Frances Alexander, 1889. Adapted for use with Anglican Prayer Beads by Laura Kelly Campbell

CELTIC PRAYER FORMS

FOR CHARITY (FROM AN OLD IRISH HOMILY)

Cross
Lord, be a bright flame before me, be a guiding star above me, be a smooth path below me, be a kindly shepherd behind me, today and for evermore. Amen.

Columba, d. 597

Invitatory

Glory be to the Father, and to the Son, and to the Holy Spirit;
As it was in the beginning, is now, and ever shall be,
world without end. Amen.

Cruciform

Our souls give thanks to you, O Lord,
for your blessings without number on heaven and earth.
And so may the blessing of the Lord of heaven and earth
be on everyone with whom we have come into contact.
For they who receive Christ's people
actually receive Christ.

An Old Irish Homily, 9th century

Weeks

1. On their possession of field and house,
2. on their property both animate and inanimate,
3. and on everyone who serves them and is obedient to them.
4. May the earth give its fruits, may the air give its rainfall,
5. may the sea give its fishes, may there be
   more grain and milk,
6. More honey and wheat for everyone whose
   goodwill we enjoy.
7. May God give them a hundredfold on this earth and the
   kingdom of heaven in the life to come.

Dismissary

God the Sender, send us.
God the Sent, come with us.

God the Strengthener of those who go, empower us,
that we may go with you
and find those who will call you Father, Son, and Holy Spirit.

Cross
Our Father, who art in heaven, hallowed be thy name;
thy kingdom come; thy will be done; on earth as it is in heaven.
Give us this day our daily bread. And forgive us our trespasses,
as we forgive those who trespass against us.
And lead us not into temptation; but deliver us from evil.
For thine is the kingdom, and the power and the glory,
for ever and ever. Amen.

BASED ON PATRICK'S BREASTPLATE

Cross
I rise today: In hope of rising to receive the reward.

Invitatory
May Christ protect me today,
so that I may have abundant reward.

Cruciform
I rise today: in power's strength, invoking the Trinity,
believing in Threeness, confessing the Oneness,
of creation's Creator.

1st Week

I rise today:

1. in the power and love of the Cherubim,
2. in the obedience of angels,
3. in the prayers of the Patriarchs,
4. in the predictions of the prophets,
5. in the preaching of Apostles,
6. in the faith of confessors,
7. in the deeds of the righteous.

2nd Week

I rise today:

1. in Heaven's might,
2. in Sun's brightness,
3. in Moon's radiance,
4. in Lightning's quickness,
5. in Wind's swiftness,
6. in Sea's depth,
7. in Earth's stability.

3rd Week

1. Hail to you, glorious Lord!
2. Aaron and Moses praised you,
3. may male and female praise you,
4. may the seven days and the stars praise you,
5. may the lower and upper air praise you,
6. may books and letters praise you,
7. and I too shall praise you, Lord of glory.

4th Week

1. Hail to you, glorious Lord!
2. May the fish in the river praise you,
3. May thought and action praise you,
4. May the sand and the earth praise you,
5. May all the good things created praise you,
6. And I too shall praise you, Lord of glory,
7. Hail to you, glorious Lord!

Dismissary

Creator of the universe, watch over us and keep us in the light of your presence. May our praise continually blend with that of all creation, until we come together to the eternal joys which you promise in love, through Jesus Christ our Lord. Amen.

Cross

Our Father, who art in heaven, hallowed be thy name;
thy kingdom come; thy will be done; on earth as it is in heaven.
Give us this day our daily bread. And forgive us our trespasses,
as we forgive those who trespass against us.
And lead us not into temptation; but deliver us from evil.
For thine is the kingdom, and the power and the glory,
for ever and ever. Amen.

Hail to You, Glorious Lord

Cross
The Father created the world by a miracle;
It is difficult to express its measure.

Invitatory
Let us adore the Lord, maker of marvelous works;
Bright heaven with its angels,
and on earth the white-waved sea.

Old Irish, 9th century

Cruciform
Almighty Creator, it is you who made the land and the sea…
The world cannot comprehend in song bright and melodious,
even though all the grass and trees should sing all your
wonders, O true Lord!

Early Welsh Prayer

1st Week
1. Hail to you, glorious Lord!
2. May chancel and church praise you,
3. may plain and hillside praise you,
4. may the three springs praise you,
5. two higher than the wind and one above the earth,
6. may darkness and light praise you,
7. and I too shall praise you, Lord of glory.

2nd Week

1. Hail to you, glorious Lord!
2. Abraham praised you, the founder of faith.
3. May life everlasting praise you,
4. may the birds and the bees praise you,
5. may the stubble and the grass praise you,
6. may the cedar and sweet fruit-tree praise you,
7. and I too shall praise you, Lord of glory.

3rd Week

I rise today:
1. with the power of God to pilot me,
2. God's strength to sustain me,
3. God's wisdom to guide me,
4. God's eye to look ahead for me, and ear to hear me,
5. God's word to speak for me,
6. God's way before me,
7. God's hand to protect me, and shield to defend me.

4th Week

1. Christ before me, Christ behind me;
2. Christ beneath me, Christ above me;
3. Christ to the right of me; Christ to the left of me;
4. Christ in the heart of all who think of me,
5. Christ on the tongue of all who speak to me,
6. Christ in the eye of all who see me,
7. Christ in the ear of all who hear me.

Dismissary

For to the Lord belongs salvation,
and to the Lord belongs salvation,
and to Christ belongs salvation.

Cross

May your salvation, Lord, be with us always. Amen.

Thirst for God

(from the prayers of Moucan, Welsh, 8th Century)

Cross

Have mercy on me, O God, have mercy on me,
forgive me, Almighty, for I have sinned.
Accept repentance from my heart,
raise up this poor one from the trash-heap.

Invitatory

If you look upon my wickedness,
I shall melt like wax in the face of fire,
like a burden of lead that weighs me down
are the sands of my sins.

Cruciform

As the hart desires a spring of living water,
so my soul thirsts for you.
My soul is like a land without water.
My bowels burned as if with fire.

May my heart burn with the fire of your love and fear,
your love and holy fear which knows not how to yield.

Weeks

Give me, Jesus, water springing into eternal life.
or the following
I wandered on the mountains, Good Shepherd,
place me upon your shoulders.

Dismissary

I have sought only my soul from the Lord,
this only I require: That I shall never thirst in eternity.

Cross

Our Father, who art in heaven, hallowed be thy name;
thy kingdom come; thy will be done; on earth as it is in heaven.
Give us this day our daily bread. And forgive us our trespasses,
as we forgive those who trespass against us.
And lead us not into temptation; but deliver us from evil.
For thine is the kingdom, and the power and the glory,
for ever and ever. Amen.

CONTRITION

Cross

Grant me tears, O Lord, to blot out my sins;
may I not cease from them, O God, until I have been purified.
Grant me contrition of heart so that I may not be in disgrace;

O Lord, protect me and grant me tears.
Old Irish

Invitatory
Glory be to the Father, and to the Son, and to the Holy Spirit;
As it was in the beginning, is now, and ever shall be,
world without end. Amen.

Cruciform
Father, I have sinned against heaven and before you:
Have mercy upon me and hear me.
I am not worthy to be called your child;
come to my aid, O God.
Make me like one of your hired servants;
forgive me and spare me my sins.
Because I greatly hunger for you,
wipe out the wickedness of my sin.
Show favor to me, Lord, a sinner;
snatch my soul from the hand of hell.
From The Prayers of Moucan, Welsh, 8th century

Weeks
We implore you, by the memory of your Cross's hallowed and
most bitter anguish, make us fear you, and make us love you,
O Christ.
Bridget, d. c. 523
or the following
Jesu, son of David, have mercy on me,
that I may open the eyes of my heart. *From The Prayers of Moucan*

Dismissary

Illustrious, compassionate Spirit, the glory of prophets,
fair soul of the comely cross of Christ, like a jewel within us,
oh cleanse us.

Iolo Goch, Welsh, 14th century

Cross

Our Father, who art in heaven, hallowed be thy name;
thy kingdom come; thy will be done; on earth as it is in heaven.
Give us this day our daily bread. And forgive us our trespasses,
as we forgive those who trespass against us.
And lead us not into temptation; but deliver us from evil.
For thine is the kingdom, and the power and the glory,
for ever and ever. Amen.